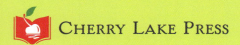

Published in the United States of America by Cherry Lake Publishing Group
Ann Arbor, Michigan
www.cherrylakepublishing.com

Reading Adviser: Beth Walker Gambro, MS, Ed., Reading Consultant, Yorkville, IL
Content Adviser: Kristin Fontichiaro, Clinical Professor, University of Michigan School of Information

Photo Credits: © CarlosBarquero/Shutterstock, cover, title page; Courtesy of Lynne Woodison, 5, 6; © Daniel Hoz/Shutterstock, 7; © Jack Frog/Shutterstock, 8; © PeopleImages.com - Yuri A, 9; © Brian Friedman/Shutterstock, 10; © Gorodenkoff/Shutterstock, 11; © Kaspars Grinvalds/Shutterstock, 12; © fizkes/Shutterstock, 13; © Monkey Business Images/Shutterstock, 15,16; 17; © Monkey Business Images/Shutterstock, 18, 20; © Kaspars Grinvalds/Shutterstock, 21; © Monkey Business Images/Shutterstock, 22; © SynthEx/Shutterstock, 23; 25; © Pixel-Shot/Shutterstock, 26; ©LightField Studios/Shutterstock, 27; © nacho roca/Shutterstock, 28; © Cast Of Thousands/Shutterstock, 30; © pics five/Shutterstock, 31

Copyright © 2025 by Cherry Lake Publishing Group

All rights reserved. No part of this book may be reproduced or utilized in any form or by any means without written permission from the publisher.

Cherry Lake Press is an imprint of Cherry Lake Publishing Group.

Library of Congress Cataloging-in-Publication Data

Names: Knutson, Julie, author.
Title: Understanding audience / written by Julie Knutson.
Description: Ann Arbor, Michigan : Cherry Lake Publishing, 2025. | Series: Take a look! Modern media literacy | Audience: Grades 4-6 | Summary: "Part of our Take a Look! Modern Media Literacy series, Understanding Audience takes readers through the process of looking critically at media to understand its audience, along with how to tailor their own media creations to specific audiences. Series closely aligned with standards from the American Association of School Librarians and the Journalism Education Association. This series gives readers a crash course in basic media literacy skills: understanding audience, perspective, persuasive appeals, author's purpose, tracing sources, and creating media content"—Provided by publisher.
Identifiers: LCCN 2024035968 | ISBN 9781668956328 (hardcover) | ISBN 9781668957172 (paperback) | ISBN 9781668958049 (ebook) | ISBN 9781668958919 (pdf)
Subjects: LCSH: Mass media—Audiences—Juvenile literature. | Media literacy—Juvenile literature.
Classification: LCC P96.A83 K58 2025 | DDC 302.23—dc23/eng/20240827
LC record available at https://lccn.loc.gov/2024035968

Cherry Lake Press would like to acknowledge the work of the Partnership for 21st Century Learning, a Network of Battelle for Kids. Please visit Battelle for Kids online for more information.

Printed in the United States of America

Note from publisher: Websites change regularly, and their future contents are outside of our control. Supervise children when conducting any recommended online searches for extended learning opportunities.

Julie Knutson (she/her) is an author and educator who lives and works in Philadelphia, PA. She's no stranger to navigating media in our modern world, and she teaches her students to do the same. Whether working with students to craft interview questions or debating designs for a classroom magazine, she also loves guiding middle schoolers through the media-making process.

CONTENTS

Chapter 1:
**Take a Look!
The Big Picture | 4**

Chapter 2:
**Break It Down!
How to Identify Audience | 14**

Chapter 3:
**Show What You Know!
Identify Audience | 24**

Do More! Extension Activity | 30
Learn More | 31
Glossary | 32
Index | 32

CHAPTER 1

Take a Look! The Big Picture

Have you ever been bored watching a cartoon for little kids? Or confused watching a show adults watch? You weren't the audience. Creators didn't make these shows for viewers like you. It's important to know who the creator thinks their audience is. It will help you figure out if it's right for you.

Consider it from a creator's perspective.

Imagine that you're learning about habitat loss in science. You're troubled by what you've discovered. You want to do something about it! You decide to write an email to the U.S. president to express your concerns.

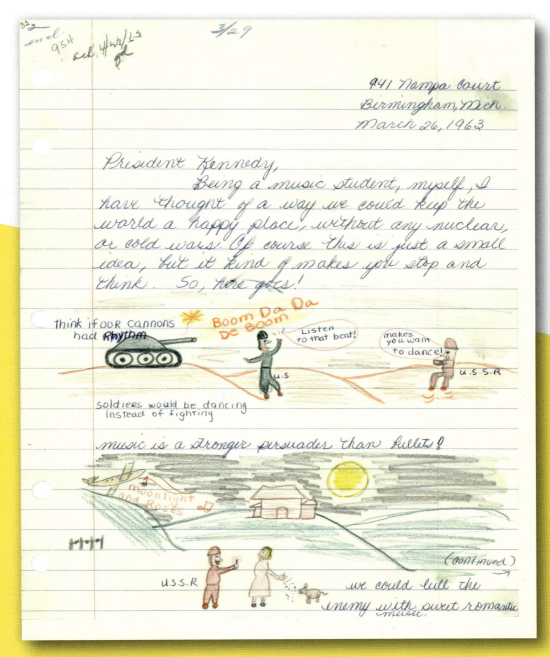

Kids have written letters to the U.S. president for decades. Take a look at this note that 11-year-old music student Lynne Woodison wrote to President John F. Kennedy in 1963. What ideas does she share? How does she use words and examples to express her thoughts?

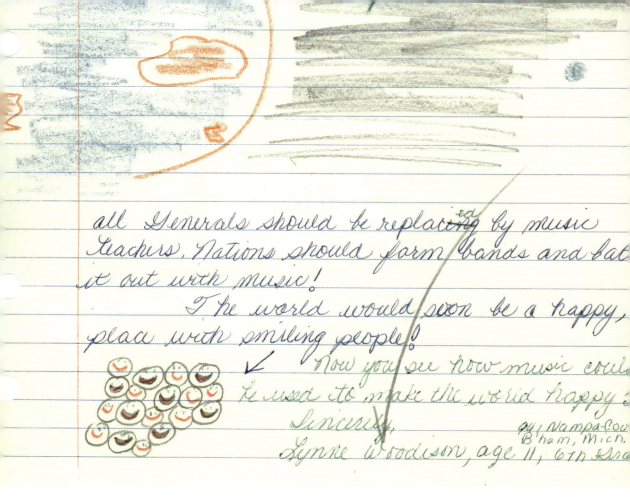

Notice how Lynne Woodison signed her letter to the president. Does it seem like a good choice given her audience?

You start the email draft. You're liking how it sounds.

Hey Prez – Can u PLZ do something about the forests? They are going away. I am worried about animals losing their homes. I love birds! I want them to have a happy habitat! I also really like dogs and cats. 🐦🐕🐈

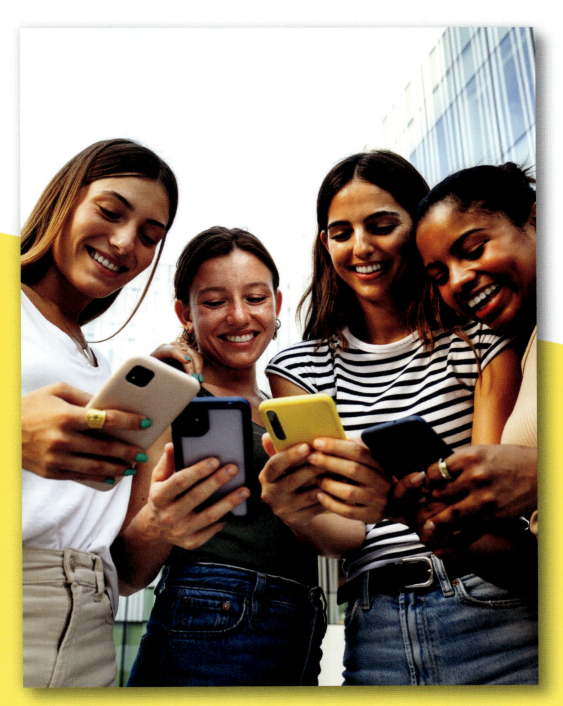

You may use slang or emojis when texting your friends. But you wouldn't use these things in all of your writing. An essay assignment your teacher reads? Not the right place for slang and emojis.

Maybe this is what you imagine when you see the word *audience*. But audiences range from one person to billions of people.

You show a draft of your email to your older sister. Her mouth drops. She puts her hand to her forehead. She pulls up a chair and explains, "This is for THE PRESIDENT OF THE UNITED STATES. That's a very different audience than writing a text to your friends!" "She's so dramatic. Sheesh."

Just what does she mean by audience? Why would you have to change what you say—and how you say it—based on who is receiving a message?

THINK & INQUIRE

People around you may change the way they speak based on their audience. Does your teacher talk to you the same way they talk to other teachers in the school? If you have a sibling, do they talk to you the same way they talk to your parents? Come up with your own questions to explore this topic.

Defining Audience

We often think of *the audience* as a large group gathered for a live performance. But audience refers to anyone that a message reaches. That can mean a single person or a room full of people or billions of YouTube viewers.

Think about a student giving a speech in class for a grade. Maybe someone is speaking at a town hall meeting about a local issue that affects them. These are

THINK & ENGAGE

Beyoncé. Taylor Swift. LeBron James. These public figures speak to global audiences of a range of ages and backgrounds. Use technology to gather information about how one of these figures talks to different audiences. How do they change the way they speak to people of different ages and backgrounds?

Who do you think the audience of this media would be?

more serious settings, or formal settings. The audiences in these settings are more formal too. But some audiences are more informal. These audiences are in a casual setting or consist of people the creator knows well. Examples would include talking with classmates at lunch or sending messages to friends on social **media**.

A creator's awareness of their audience's background knowledge, experiences, and interests allows them to create effective media content. The words they choose,

The next time you watch a show, pay attention to the commercials or ads. Do they seem geared toward adults or kids? Men or women?

the evidence they provide and the images they feature all matter! They are all selected with an audience in mind. It's helpful to know how to identify the audience of a piece of media. Knowing what audience the creator is trying to reach can tell you about the content.

AUDIENCE RESEARCH: A BIG BUSINESS

Toy maker Mattel. Tech giant Tesla. These companies spend billions of dollars to get to know their audiences. They do this through **market research**. This research helps companies gather information about their audience. It tells them what people buy, why they buy it, and how they buy it.

How does market research work? Sometimes it's by talking to groups of people called **focus groups**. Researchers observe these groups to learn their wants, needs, and mindsets.

Another side of market research is all about numbers. Social media numbers. Sales numbers. Numbers from surveys. These numbers help companies make decisions. Maybe thousands of people watch an ad video for an upcoming product. Then 700 people click on a link to go to the product's website. This shows companies how many people may buy the product.

CHAPTER 2

Break It Down! How to Identify Audience

Get to Know Media's Audience

Meet 7th grader Viv. Viv is passionate about her school. She wants it to be a place that builds community. She thinks it would be great if her school could hold community events.

There is a student election coming up. Students in her middle school will vote for one school council president. There are two candidates. Viv isn't sure who she wants to vote for. Each candidate made a video. Teachers sent the videos out to parents. Students have been encouraged to watch these videos to decide how to cast their vote.

Viv's mom shares the candidate videos with her. Viv is ready to review this media.

Viv opens the videos and starts watching. She keeps the audience in mind. The audience a candidate targets will tell her a lot about them and the content they've made. She'll also be able to decide if the candidate is for her.

Looking Closely at Media Messages

Viv has studied historical advertisements in history class. She knows there are four things to look for when identifying an audience:

- Format
- Examples and Images
- Word Choice
- **Tone**

She starts the first video. The candidate is an 8th grader. In his video, he shows clips of last year's boys' basketball team. He references some inside jokes his team had last year. He talks about how the team can make this year's state championships. He ends the video with "Vote for me! I'll get buckets all day for our school!"

- **Format:** Viv considers the **format**. She knows her classmates watch a lot of videos on social media. This format would speak to most 6th through 8th graders in their school.

Viv keeps an open mind but starts to get the feeling she might not be the target audience for this first candidate's video.

- **Examples and Images:** This candidate featured video clips of last year's boys' basketball team. It seems like he's trying to reach boys, boys who play sports, and boys who play basketball, specifically. Viv doesn't fall into any of these categories.

- **Word Choice:** This candidate included inside jokes. Viv didn't understand them. He also included the phrase "get buckets" in his **campaign** slogan. His audience? The basketball team and students who understand basketball slang.

- **Tone:** The tone of this candidate's message was humorous and informal. She thinks this tone would speak to most 6th through 8th graders in her school.

Viv thinks about format, examples and images, word choice, and tone for the next video as well. It will help her identify the audience pretty quickly.

GROW & INQUIRE

It's helpful for an audience to ask, "What is this maker communicating?" and "What does this maker want people to do after hearing their message?" How could asking these questions help you interact with media content that's a good fit for you?

Based on what Viv found, she thinks this candidate ignored her and students like her. She doesn't think the candidate who created this video will have her best interests in mind. She decides to move on to the other candidate.

The next video begins. The candidate is a 6th-grade girl. Her video shows pictures of a community service project she did with her friends. This candidate thinks community service can build a great community inside and outside of school. She also talks about a new student-run tutoring program. She thinks it will help students see the power they have to help each other. She ends her video with, "Vote for me and strong community!"

When she's done watching, Viv pauses to write down some of her thoughts. She compares the two videos. She compares their audiences.

- **Format:** Viv skips this one—the format is the same as the first candidate's.

- **Examples and Images:** This candidate had pictures of her friend group. They were doing community service. It seemed like she was trying to reach people who care about community service.

- **Word Choice:** This candidate used simple language. It would be easy for any student in her school to understand.

- **Tone:** The tone of this candidate's message was more serious than the last video. But it was still pretty informal—just right for students in her school.

AI AND AUDIENCE

Generative artificial intelligence (GenAI) is often used to tailor ads and content to specific audiences online. Online stores can use this. Social media can use this. These GenAI programs collect a lot of data about what people click on and search for. The programs then "get to know" a person by looking for patterns in the data. Is the person a football fan? Are they passionate about graphic novels? Do they have a dog with allergies? The GenAI programs can then recommend specific ads and content.

Recommended videos? Ads on social media? Recommended accounts to follow? All of these things may be the result of GenAI sifting through your data. Companies are paying big money to make sure they reach you—their audience.

Be aware of the recommended content that pops up online. It is likely recommended based on your personal online use. You can choose if you want to click on it or not.
You have the power!

Viv feels like she's now able to make an informed decision. Being able to identify the audience of the two videos helped her.

Based on her findings, Viv thinks she knows the audience of the second video. She thinks it includes everyone at her school who wants a strong community. Viv is part of this audience. She thinks even the boys' basketball team would be included in this group! She believes the second candidate will have her best interests in mind. She knows who has her vote.

Viv knows she can apply this knowledge to other media she watches and hears. She already knows she'll use what she's learned the next time she's on YouTube! She can identify the audience. This can tell her more about the creator and the content of a media message. Then she can decide if the media is right for her.

SHARE & COLLABORATE

Creators communicate with audiences for many reasons. These include expressing ideas, informing people, explaining how things work, and persuading people to act. Talk about problems in your community with a friend or family member. Is there a problem you both want to solve? Discuss what media you could create to persuade people to take action.

CHAPTER 3

Show What You Know! Identify Audience

Viv enjoyed watching media made by students in her school. Most media you read or watch will not be made by students at your school. Most will be found online. Some creators do you a favor. They invite specific audiences. They might say, "If you're new to gardening, you're in the right place!" Other forms of media are not as obvious, but you can follow the same steps Viv did to understand who a piece of media is for.

The format of media matters because different audiences engage with media in different ways. Social media platforms even have data on the age ranges of their users. Is the format a TikTok or Instagram Reel? The audience is likely young. Is it a newspaper opinion piece? The audience is likely older adults. Short YouTube videos may be targeted to young viewers. Long YouTube videos may skew to older adults.

Talking to classmates, friends, and family about media may help you identify its intended audience.

Remember that there is media online and offline. Books, papers, magazines, and print ads are all still media people use daily.

26

A more serious setting like a debate tournament? The speaker will likely be formal with their verbal arguments. This can help you identify the intended audience.

Age ranges are just one way to define an audience. Other categories may be if they are wealthy or need to save money. Even geography can define an audience.

An audience's values may also define how media is made for that group. Examples and images may play on the group's beliefs, values, or even **biases**. They may be used to create fear in an audience unfamiliar with the topic.

Word choice and tone can also help identify who the media was made for and what the creator thinks their audience will like and respond to.

Editing is a big part of the media-making process. It's good to fix and change things to better suit your audience.

Remember that email to the president you started? Understanding audience doesn't just help you understand media, but create it, too! You decide to use more formal language in your email to the president. You begin:

Dear President of the United States,

Thank you for taking the time to read my letter. I am a young citizen concerned about the issue of habitat loss . . .

Your sister reads over your shoulder. "Much better," she says. You smile.

INFLUENCERS AND AUDIENCE

On an average day—whether surfing YouTube or shopping at the grocery store—you'll see more than 4,000 ads. For marketers, YOU are a key audience. On social media alone, including Instagram, TikTok, Snapchat, and YouTube, companies spent more than $11 billion marketing products to children and teens in 2022.

One way that marketers target kids and teens is through **influencers**. Influencers are online personalities. They are masters of understanding their audience because, well, they're typically members of the group that they're addressing!

Whether "unboxing" a new toy or promoting a skin care product, the words, images, and strategies that they use are part of a vocabulary they share with their audience. In doing so, they make their pitches feel authentic to the people receiving their message.

Do More!
Extension Activity

We opened our exploration of an audience with a not-so-stellar email for the U.S. president. In the end, the email became much more formal. Think about the information presented in this book. Then create a piece of media for an elected official about an issue that matters to YOU. Maybe it's school safety. Or endangered species. Or air quality. The choice is yours.

Once you've picked your topic, consider this list to craft an on-point message:

- **Choose the format of your media.**
- **Learn about what matters to your audience. You can look at past speeches, press releases, or websites with an adult. Use examples and images that reflect what you learn.**
- **Use words and language that will appeal to your audience and that your audience will understand. Avoid slang an adult likely won't know.**
- **Create a tone that reflects how you want your message received. Do you want to make something funny that makes your audience think? Do you want to make something serious that helps your audience act quickly?**

Addressing these issues in advance will help you say what you need to say AND share what you want to share!

Learn More

Books

Berne, Emma Carlson. *Understanding Advertising.* North Mankato, MN: Capstone, 2019.

Down, Susan Brophy. *Power and Persuasion in Media and Advertising.* New York City, NY: Crabtree, 2018.

On the Web

Search this online source with an adult:

- YouTube—How to Write for Your Audience Writing Video for Kids | Teaching Without Frills

Glossary

audience (AH-dee-uhnts) a person or group who hears or sees something

biases (BIE-uh-seez) prejudice in favor of or against a thing, person, or group campaign (kam-PAYN) series of actions performed to reach a specific goal

focus groups (FOH-kuhs GROOPS) groups of people who participate in studies and trials for new products

format (FOR-mat) how something is arranged or organized

generative artificial intelligence (JEH-nuh-ruh-tive ar-tuh-FIH-shuhl in-TEH-luh-juhns) computer programs that input data from sources on the internet and then output different combinations of that data

influencers (IN-floo-uhn-suhrz) people who promote goods and services using social media

market research (MAHR-kuht REE-suhrch) information that helps companies decide how to change or promote their goods and services

media (MEE-dee-uh) means of communicating information to large numbers of people, including television, newspapers, magazines, and radio

tone (TOHN) the style of writing or speaking used to achieve a result or communicate an emotion

Index

activities, 30
advertising
   audience identification, 12
   audience research and data, 13, 21, 29
artificial intelligence (AI), 21
audience
   communication considerations, 4–7, 9–11, 21, 23–28
   defining, 8–9
   identification, 11–12, 14–24, 30
   market research and data, 13, 21

content
   audience identification, 11–12, 16–21, 23, 30
   creation, 24–27, 29–30

election communications, 14–20, 22–23

focus groups, 13
formal vs. informal communication
   friends, 6–7, 9–10
   political, 4–6, 10, 17, 20, 28, 30
   school, 7, 9–10, 17, 20
formats, communication, 16, 26, 30

influencers, 29

language use
   audience matching, 4, 6, 9–12, 17, 20, 27
   letter writing, 4–6, 28
   texting, 6–7
letters to the president, 4–6, 28, 30

market research, 13

political communication
   election campaigns, 14–20, 22–23
   letters to the president, 4–6, 28, 30
   public forums, 10, 30
print media, 26
public figures, 4–6, 10, 28

school communication
   appropriateness, 7, 9–10
   audience inclusion, 14–20, 22–23
slang, 7, 17
social media
   advertising and data, 13, 21, 29
   audiences, 16, 21
   influencers, 29
   informal speech, 7, 10

targeted advertising, 13, 21, 29
texting, 6–7
tone appropriateness, 4, 6–7, 10, 17, 20, 27